FOCUS ON ELEMENTARY

3rd Edition

Rebecca W. Keller, PhD

Real Science-4-Kids

Illustrations: Janet Moneymaker

Focus On Elementary Geology Student Textbook—3rd Edition (softcover)
ISBN 978-1-941181-39-3

Published by Gravitas Publications Inc.
www.gravitaspublications.com
www.realscience4kids.com

GRAVITAS
PUBLICATIONS

Contents

Chapter 1 What Is Geology?

1.1 Introduction

In this book we will take a look at the building block of science called geology. Geology is the study of the Earth. By studying the Earth, scientists attempt to understand what Earth is made of, how Earth came into being, how Earth has changed in the past, how it is changing now, and our role as we live on Earth.

Do you ever pick up rocks and wonder how they were made and what they are made of? Do you sometimes look at mountains and wonder how they were formed?

Have you wondered what's at the bottom of the ocean? Have you noticed how weather affects the landscape? Do you wonder why certain birds and wild animals live near you and others don't? These are all questions that are explored by scientists who study geology.

1.2 History of Geology

Depending on where you live, when you go outside and walk around, you'll see many different features of Earth. You might see mountains or rivers. You might see fields of dirt or fields of grass. You might see lakes or oceans, mesas or glaciers, forests or prairies.

Ancient people also saw many of the same features you see. Although lakes come and go and rivers might change course, many of the features you see today are the same features ancient people would have seen.

One of the first people to study Earth's features was the Greek philosopher Theophrastus who lived from about 371-287 BCE.

Theophrastus was a student of Aristotle, a Greek philosopher who was one of the first to study plants and animals. Like Aristotle, Theophrastus was interested in science. He studied rocks and explored what happens when rocks are heated.

THEOPHRASTUS
371-287 BCE

Many of the first geologists also asked questions about how the Earth came into being and how many years the Earth has existed. All of these questions shaped the modern science we now call geology.

1.3 Modern Geology

Modern geologists continue to study rocks and what rocks are made of. They also ask questions about how mountains, rivers, and glaciers form. Modern geologists have an advantage over ancient geologists because modern geologists can use chemistry and physics to better understand how things work.

There are different kinds of modern geologists. Some modern geologists focus on the chemistry of Earth. These geologists are called geochemists. Geochemists study how atoms and molecules make rocks, soils, minerals, and fuels.

Other modern geologists focus on the structure of Earth. These geologists are called structural geologists. Structural geologists study how Earth is put together and how it changes. They are interested in how rocks change and what makes mountains and valleys.

There are also modern geologists who study how humans affect the water, air, and land quality of Earth. These geologists study Earth's environment and are called environmental geologists.

1.4 Everyday Geology

Even though you may not be a geologist yet, you can learn about the Earth by simply observing what happens around you.

What happens when it rains? Do the roads flood? Do you get mud slides, or does a river find a new path? What happens in the hot sun? Do you observe mud forming cracks or rocks crumbling? Have you ever been in an earthquake? Did you feel the ground move?

Paying attention to where you live, what happens during storms, and how the land around you changes over time are activities you can do every day.

1.5 Summary

○ Geology is the study of Earth.

○ The first geologists looked at rocks and minerals and asked questions about how Earth came into being.

○ Geochemists are modern geologists who study how atoms and molecules form Earth.

○ Structural geologists look at how Earth is put together.

○ Environmental geologists look at changes in the quality of the water, the air, and the land on Earth.

1.6 Some Things to Think About

○ Go outside and look for rocks. How many different kinds can you see? Are they different colors? Are some smoother than others? What else can you notice?

○ Go outside for a walk and look at what is around you. Write some questions about parts of the Earth you see and would like to find out more about.

○ Which area of geology sounds most interesting to you? What would you like to learn about?

> Geochemistry
>
> Structural geology
>
> Environmental geology

○ Think about times when it has rained really hard. What changes to the Earth did you notice?

Chapter 2 Geologist's Toolbox

2.1 Introduction

Geologists are scientists who use special tools to study Earth. Some tools are basic, like hammers and lenses, and some tools are more advanced, like seismographs and submarines.

There are different tools for different types of geologists. Some geologists study what things are made of and may use test tubes and chemicals to test minerals and rocks. Some geologists study how things are put together and might use hammers and microscopes to examine layers of sediments and inside rocks.

Because there are many different types of geologists, there are many different types of tools in a geologist's toolbox.

2.2 Brief History

It's difficult to know exactly what the first geology tool was and when it was invented. It is clear from a variety of ancient texts that early geologists were curious about what was inside rocks and beneath layers of dirt, and they likely used simple tools such as hammers and shovels to examine rocks and minerals.

THEOPHRASTUS
372-287 BCE

Recall from Chapter 1 that Theophrastus was a Greek philosopher who studied rocks and explored what happens when rocks are heated. Theophrastus wrote a book called *On Stones* in which he describes the color, hardness, and smoothness of a variety of both common and rare stones. Many of these stones were found on the ground, in streams, and by mining.

It is also clear from writings of Theophrastus that he explored the nature of stones by performing various experiments. By using fire, he could observe which stones melted or changed color when burned. Theophrastus also used acids to examine which stones would dissolve and which would withstand these chemical tests.

2.3 Basic Tools: Hammers and Lenses

Three types of rock hammers used by geologists are: the pointed tip rock hammer, the chisel edge rock hammer, and the crack hammer.

A pointed tip rock hammer has one end that comes to a point. The other end has a head that is flat and square. Pointed tip rock hammers are also called rock picks, and they are generally used by geologists when they are working with hard rocks. Geologists often use the pointy tip to dig fossil samples out of rocks and the square end to crack open a rock to see what's inside.

A chisel edge rock hammer has one end that is flat and broad like a chisel rather than being pointy. The other end is a square head. The chisel end is used to split layers of soft rock. The square head is used to crack open rocks.

A crack hammer has two blunt ends. It is usually heavier than either a pointed tip rock hammer or a chisel edge rock hammer. Its heaviness can make it easier for geologists to break rocks open.

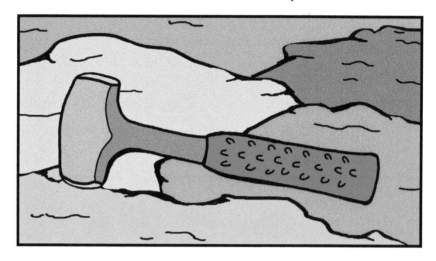

Once a geologist breaks a rock open with a rock hammer, is there a way to get a better look at what's inside? To

better see the features of the inside of a rock, geologists often use a hand lens. A hand lens is a small magnifier that folds into a holder, making it compact and easy to carry. A hand lens can be carried in a pocket or on a string around the neck.

A hand lens magnifies a rock, making it easier to see. With a hand lens, a geologist can look at the details of a rock. This can help determine what the rock is made of.

2.4 Advanced Geology Tools

Modern geologists use a variety of advanced tools to study Earth's rocks, minerals, soils, and Earth's activity. Computers, satellites, radios, and other modern technologies play a very important role in how geologists collect and analyze data.

A global positioning system or GPS is an electronic device that has greatly changed how geologists map and study Earth's surface. A GPS device receives signals from a network of satellites orbiting the Earth. The GPS unit then uses this data to calculate its location on the Earth. Many GPS devices are small enough to be easily tucked into a backpack or pocket. Geologists use GPS devices to help them do things such as navigate, create geographical maps, locate specific landmarks, and determine property lines.

Another advanced technology that has helped geologists map Earth's surface is the geographic information system or GIS. A GIS is a system that uses computers to gather and sort different types of geographical data. The data can then be used to create maps that help geologist examine mountains, rivers, volcanoes, earthquakes, and even geological features beneath the ocean!

2.5 Summary

○ Geologists use both basic and advanced tools.

○ Many geologists use basic tools such as rock hammers and hand lenses.

○ Geologists also use advanced electronic tools such as the GPS (global positioning system).

○ Computers play an important role in the study of geology. Geologists use computer systems, such as GIS (geographic information system), to study Earth's surface.

2.6 Some Things to Think About

○ Find a rock that is broken, or break a rock with a hammer. What does the inside look like? Is it the same on the inside as it is on the outside? Do you see crystals? Different colored layers? Fossils? Other features? Describe what you see. Use a hand lens or magnifying glass to observe more details.

○ Where have you found the most interesting rocks?

○ What does your favorite rock look like? Why is it your favorite?

○ If you used a rock hammer to open a rock, what do you think you might learn?

○ If you were to use GIS to study the ocean floor, what do you think you might find?

Chapter 3: What Is Earth Made Of?

3.1 Introduction

If you walk outside, do you notice where you live? If you live in the country, do you notice the trees and grass? If you live in a city, do you notice the buildings and streets?

If you look down, do you notice the ground? If you live in a city, do you notice how much of the ground is covered up with streets or pavement? If you live in the country, do you notice if the ground has grass, rocks, or dirt?

When you notice the ground with the rocks, dirt, grass, and trees, you are noticing the Earth. The Earth is where you live.

But what is the Earth made of? What is dirt? What are rocks? Why do grass and trees grow in dirt? How deep does the dirt go? How many kinds of rocks are there? What is below the rocks and dirt? More rocks? Trees? Chocolate syrup?

In this chapter we will learn about what the Earth is made of.

3.2 Rocks and Minerals

The crust is the outer part of Earth and is where we live. The crust is mostly made of rock. If you go outside and start digging in the ground with a shovel, you will eventually hit some type of rock.

What is the difference between a rock and a tree? Trees are living things. Rocks are not living things. Rocks do not move like living things. Rocks do not grow like living things, and rocks do not multiply like living things.

Living things are made mostly of carbon, but rocks are made mostly of silicon. Silicon and carbon are atoms (also called elements). Because rocks are made mostly from silicon and living things are made mostly from carbon, rocks are very different from living things.

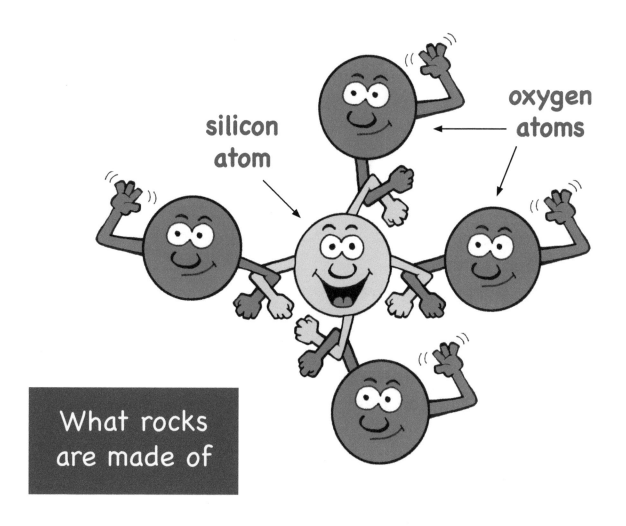

silicon atom

oxygen atoms

What rocks are made of

All rocks come from magma, which is molten (melted) rock deep inside the Earth. Magma is made mostly of the elements silicon and oxygen. Rocks form when the magma cools and mixes with other elements, like magnesium, iron, or aluminum.

When magma cools very slowly, the atoms in the magma have a chance to line up in an orderly fashion. When this happens, the material that is formed is called a mineral.

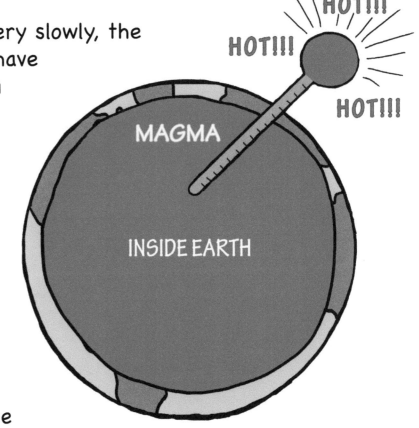

There are many different kinds of minerals. One common mineral found in rocks is quartz. Quartz can be clear, pink, purple, or other colors.

Mica is also a mineral. Mica is soft and looks like thin, layered paper. You can peel mica sheets away from each other.

Calcite is another mineral found in rocks. Calcite is made of calcium and oxygen and forms beautiful crystals that come in different colors.

Minerals

Quartz   Mica   Calcite

Some minerals are used in jewelry. Rubies are a brilliant red-colored mineral made of aluminum and oxygen. Emeralds are a different type of mineral made of aluminum, beryllium, silicon, and oxygen. Emeralds have a deep green color. Both rubies and emeralds are hard to find, and that is why jewelry made with them is often expensive.

Ruby Crystal

There are also many different kinds of rocks. There are rocks that are formed deep inside the Earth, and there are rocks that form on the surface of the Earth. There are also rocks that have been changed from one type of rock into another type of rock. The different types of rocks are called igneous, sedimentary, and metamorphic. Minerals are the building blocks of all these types of rocks.

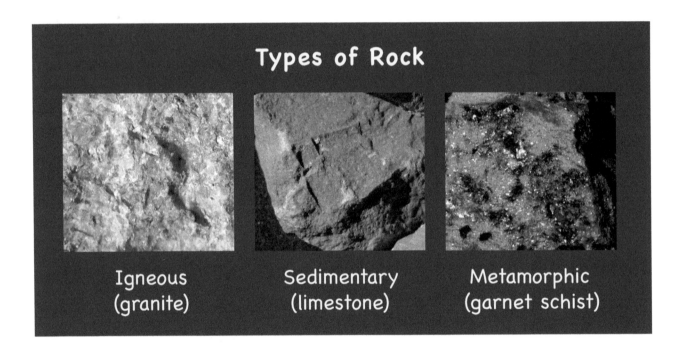

Types of Rock

Igneous
(granite)

Sedimentary
(limestone)

Metamorphic
(garnet schist)

Igneous rocks are the most plentiful type of rock. Igneous rocks are formed when molten magma inside the Earth cools and hardens. Granite is one kind of igneous rock, and it has a lot of quartz in it.

Sedimentary rocks are formed from bits of rocks and other materials left behind by wind or water. As these materials pile on top of each other, layers form. These layers are pressed tightly together, turning the materials into rock.

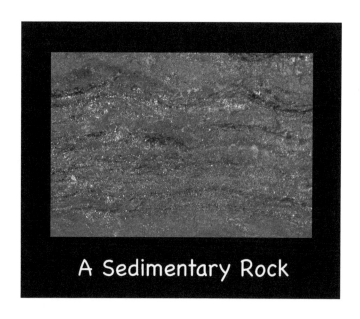

A Sedimentary Rock

A Metamorphic Rock

Metamorphic rocks are those that have changed from one type of rock into another. Very high heat and pressure cause these changes. Igneous rocks and sedimentary rocks can be changed into metamorphic rocks. Even metamorphic rocks can be changed into other metamorphic rocks!

3.3 Dirt

When you go outside and dig a hole in the ground, you not only find rocks but you also find dirt. Dirt is made of rocks, plants, minerals, and even small animals!

There are many different types of dirt. Some dirt is sandy and light in color. Other dirt is moist and dark in color. Have you ever wondered why some parts of the world are used for growing food and other parts of the world are not? That's because some dirt is good for growing plants and other dirt is not.

Dirt is also called soil. Dirt and soil come mainly from rocks. Because different parts of the Earth have different kinds of rocks, there are different types of soil in different places.

3.4 Summary

○ The Earth is made mostly of rock.

○ All rocks come from magma.

○ Minerals form when magma cools slowly, allowing the atoms to line up in an orderly fashion.

○ Dirt is called soil. It is made mostly from rocks and contains materials that come from plants, minerals, and animals.

3.5 Some Things to Think About

○ Look around outside. Can you find a rock that might be a layered sedimentary rock? Can you find a rock that might have tiny bits of sparkly quartz in it? Can you find a rock that is very smooth? Can you find a rock that is very rough? Make a list of what you find!

○ Go outside and look at dirt. Feel it too! Can you find different colors of dirt? Can you find different kinds of dirt? Describe what you find.

○ Find a place where you can dig a little hole in the ground. What can you observe about what dirt is made of? Do you think if you could dig a really deep hole, the dirt would look the same at the bottom of the hole as at the top?

Chapter 4 Our Earth

4.1 Shape of Earth

What is the shape of Earth? Is it round like a circle? Is it spherical like a ball? Is it flat like a pancake? Is it square like a block? Does it look like a pumpkin or an eggplant?

When you take a walk around your neighborhood, Earth seems flat. As you go to the park or walk to the store, you don't slide off the ground and you don't lean to the left or right. When you walk on a hill, you go up and then down again. You can walk for many miles and the Earth will seem flat.

However, if you look at the Earth from an airplane or from a boat at sea, you'll discover that the Earth is not flat, but curved. If you looked at Earth from a spaceship, you would discover that Earth is shaped like a ball.

But Earth is not shaped like a perfectly round ball. The middle of the Earth is pushed out a little, and the top and bottom are slightly flattened. The Earth is shaped like a slightly smashed ball!

The top part of Earth is called the North Pole, and the bottom part of Earth is called the South Pole. The middle of Earth is called the equator.

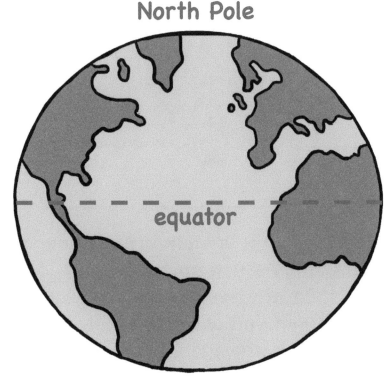

North Pole

equator

South Pole

4.2 Size of Earth

It's hard to imagine that we walk, run, and live on a planet that's shaped like a ball. If you live at the middle of Earth, near the equator, do you feel like you are standing sideways? If you go to the South Pole do you feel upside down? If you go to the North Pole do you feel right-side up?

In fact, if you go anywhere on the Earth, you don't feel upside down or sideways. You always feel right-side up.

Why does Earth seem flat if it is actually a curved ball? And why do we always feel upright even when we are at the South Pole or on the equator?

Many years ago some people were afraid to travel too far out to sea. They thought the Earth was flat and that they

would fall off the edge if they went too far! It made sense to them because the Earth felt flat.

What they didn't know is that the Earth is very large. The Earth is so large that we can't feel the Earth's curve when

we walk or run. The Earth is so large that we can't tell if we are on the top, on the bottom, or on the side.

The Earth is about 40,200 kilometers (25,000 miles) around. It would take you more than a year to walk around the Earth! That's how big Earth is. Because Earth is so large, it feels flat when we walk, run, work, or play. But the Earth is really a huge ball.

4.3 Parts of Earth

Earth has different parts. You know that when you walk outside, you step on rocks and dirt. Rocks, minerals, and dirt make up the outer part of Earth. Rocks, minerals, and dirt also make up the ocean floor.

But what is beneath the dirt and the ocean? What is inside the Earth? Is it rocks, minerals, and dirt like the outer part? Or is it chocolate syrup, liquid gold, or melted cheese?

Scientists have no way to actually see what's below the outer surface of Earth, but by studying volcanoes and earthquakes, scientists can come up with some ideas about what lies below the surface.

4.4 Earth's Layers

Earth is a rock planet, which means that it is made mostly of rocks.

If scientists were able to cut the Earth in half, they think they would see at least three different layers. This means that the outer surface of Earth, where you walk, is different from the part just below it.

The crust is the outermost layer of Earth. The crust is made up of rocks, minerals, and soil. The crust is very hard. This hard outer layer supports you when you walk and it supports buildings. The crust also holds the oceans. The crust is relatively thin compared to the layers below it, and it makes up only a small part of Earth.

Below the crust is the mantle. Scientists think the mantle is much thicker than the crust and is made of layers. Scientists believe the outer part of the mantle is hard and rocky. The inner part of the mantle is thought to be softer and hotter.

Scientists think this inner part of the mantle might be more like gooey peanut butter and made of melted rock called magma. Scientists think that the magma

in the mantle does not always stay in the same place but moves around!

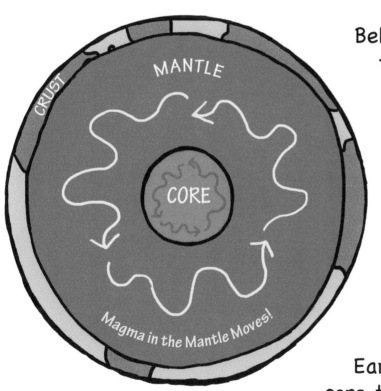

Below the mantle and in the very center of Earth is the core. Scientists believe that the outer part of the core is made of molten iron and nickel and the inner part of the core is solid and made mostly of iron. The core is very heavy.

Earth's crust, mantle, and core together are called the geosphere.

4.5 Summary

○ The Earth is made of layers.

○ The main layers of the Earth are the crust, the mantle, and the core.

○ The crust is the hard, rocky, outermost layer of Earth.

○ The mantle is below the crust. Most of the mantle is soft and the outer part closest to the crust is hard.

○ The core is at the center of the Earth. The inner part of the core is likely solid.

4.6 Some Things to Think About

○ What do you think it would be like to live on a planet shaped like a pumpkin? What if the planet was shaped like a jack o'lantern?

○ Do you think air and ocean travel would be different if Earth were flat? If it were square? Why or why not?

○ If you could dig a really, really deep hole in your backyard and another really, really deep hole at the bottom of the ocean, do you think you would find different things as you dig the two holes?
Why or why not?

○ If you wanted to tell your friends about the different layers of Earth, how would you describe them?

Chapter 5 Earth Is Active

5.1 Introduction

The Earth is an active planet. It is always changing. For example, we can see the surface of the Earth change with the seasons. In the spring and summer some parts of Earth

can be covered with flowers and green grass. In the winter, these same parts might be covered with snow.

You might think that the Earth's crust doesn't change because it is hard and rocky, but it changes every day. There are volcanoes, earthquakes, storms, and flowing rivers that continuously change the Earth's crust.

Geologists study how Earth has changed by looking at rocks, dirt layers, mountains, and other features. Geologists also look at volcanoes, earthquakes, weather, and other things that cause changes on Earth.

5.2 Volcanoes Erupt

Volcanoes can be very exciting. Sometimes when a volcano erupts, a whole mountaintop will come off in a huge explosion!

Volcanoes happen when magma in the mantle pushes up through a weak spot in the crust and comes to the surface of the Earth.

Magma is formed when the rocks and minerals in the mantle melt because the weight of the crust is pushing down on them, creating heat and pressure.

Pressure happens when you squeeze something and it doesn't have anywhere to go. For example, if you keep the lid on

your toothpaste and squeeze the bottom of the tube, you will create pressure in the tube. If the top suddenly pops off, the toothpaste will explode! If there is a crack in the wall of the toothpaste tube, the toothpaste will squirt out the side.

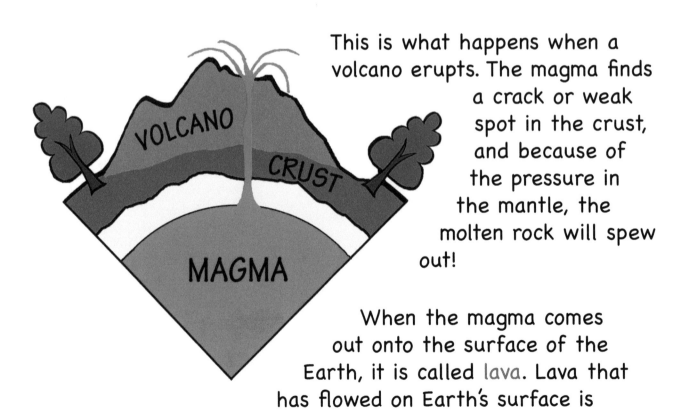

This is what happens when a volcano erupts. The magma finds a crack or weak spot in the crust, and because of the pressure in the mantle, the molten rock will spew out!

When the magma comes out onto the surface of the Earth, it is called lava. Lava that has flowed on Earth's surface is responsible for many interesting features that are created when the lava cools and forms hard rock. Sometimes lava flows form whole islands. The Hawaiian Islands, for example, are a group of islands made from lava flows.

Volcanoes can form mountains of different shapes and sizes. Some volcanoes form gently sloping mountains over long periods of time. These volcanoes are called shield volcanoes

because their long, sloping sides make them resemble the shape of a shield. Shield volcanoes form when very thin layers of lava flow out in all directions. A mountain is formed as the layers build up on top of each other. Shield volcanoes can be several miles long with sides that slope very gradually. The Hawaiian Islands are a series of shield volcanoes.

Volcanoes can also form mountains with steeper sides. Cone volcanoes are cone-shaped because the magma spurts out more quickly and is thicker than the magma that forms shield

volcanoes. Also, more rocks and dirt are scattered. The rocks and dirt pile up along the sides of the volcano, making the sides steeper and steeper. Interestingly, cone volcanoes are often found on the edges of shield volcanoes.

Volcanoes can also form dome-shaped mountains. Lava dome mountains are often round in shape and look like a cereal bowl turned upside down! The magma that comes from dome volcanoes is very thick and doesn't flow very far away from the center.

5.3 Earthquakes Shake

Earthquakes can also be very exciting and even scary if you happen to be near one when it happens. Earthquakes occur because sections of the Earth's crust suddenly move. Recall that the hard, rocky crust lies on top of the hard outer part of the mantle, and the hard outer part of the mantle lies on top of the inner part of the mantle that is soft like peanut butter.

Scientists think that the outer part of the mantle is cracked into huge pieces called plates that fit together like a big puzzle. These pieces, or plates, float on the part of the mantle that is soft like peanut butter.

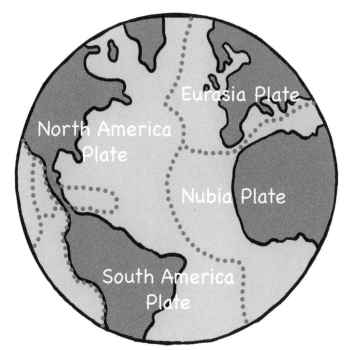

Earthquakes happen suddenly and are usually over within a few minutes. If the earthquake is small, you might feel the floor move, and you might hear a sound like a nearby train. If the earthquake is large, the whole ground moves and buildings and trees may fall. Sometimes after a big earthquake, several smaller earthquakes occur.

When plates move against each other, one section might move upward and the other might move downward. Or the sections might slide past one another. When these things happen, there is movement of the land on either side of the line that is between the two sections.

Let's imagine you have a street in front of your house that separates your yard from your neighbor's yard. Imagine that your house sits on one section of the Earth and your neighbor's house sits on a different section of the Earth. If these two sections move past one another, it's possible that your neighbor from across the street is now your next-door neighbor!

5.4 Summary

○ The Earth's surface is constantly changing.

○ Volcanoes and earthquakes change Earth's crust.

○ Volcanoes happen when magma in the mantle pushes up through a weak spot in the Earth's surface.

○ Earthquakes happen when sections of the Earth's surface move.

5.5 Some Things to Think About

○ What are some ways that you have seen the Earth change?

○ How do you think volcanoes make mountains that are different shapes?

○ Why do you think having a soft layer in the mantle under the plates helps create earthquakes?

Chapter 6 Earth's Spheres

6.1 Introduction

If you go outside and walk around in your backyard, you will notice a variety of features that make up the place on Earth where you live.

When you jump up and down, you can feel the hard rock surface below your feet. If you have a shovel, you might dig a little way below the surface and observe dirt, rocks, and minerals. This is the "rock part" of Earth, called the crust. The crust and all of the layers of Earth below the crust together are called the geosphere.

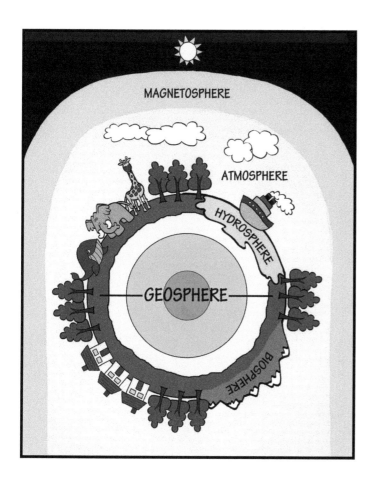

When you inhale and exhale, you feel your lungs fill with oxygen and then release carbon dioxide. This is the "air part" of Earth called the atmosphere.

If you walk on the grass or kneel down to examine tiny ants taking off with crumbs from your peanut butter sandwich, you are looking at the "biology part" of Earth called the biosphere.

If it starts to rain on you while you are looking at the ants scurrying on the ground and carrying your sandwich crumbs, you are experiencing the "water part" of Earth called the hydrosphere.

And finally, if you use a compass to find your way home, you are interacting with the "magnetic part" of Earth called the magnetic field which is within the magnetosphere. The magnetosphere is the area surrounding Earth in space where Earth's magnetic field interacts with gases given off by the Sun.

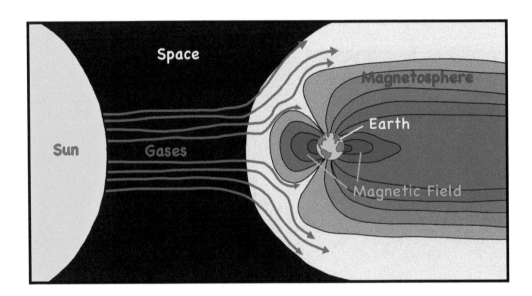

The geosphere, atmosphere, biosphere, hydrosphere, and magnetosphere can be studied both separately and together. As a whole, they make up this planet we know as Earth.

6.2 Why Spheres?

Notice that all of these names end in the term sphere. The word sphere refers to a ball-shaped object. The Earth is a ball-shaped or *spherical* object in space.

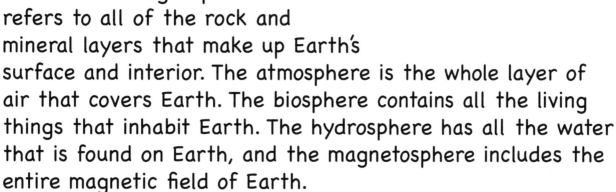

When geologists talk about any of the "spheres" of Earth, they are talking about a whole part, or layer, that encircles the Earth. The geosphere refers to all of the rock and mineral layers that make up Earth's surface and interior. The atmosphere is the whole layer of air that covers Earth. The biosphere contains all the living things that inhabit Earth. The hydrosphere has all the water that is found on Earth, and the magnetosphere includes the entire magnetic field of Earth.

When geologists study a particular part of a layer of the Earth, they use words that describe specific features. For example, mountains, rocks, and the ocean floor are different parts of the geosphere. Oceans, lakes, and glaciers are different parts of the hydrosphere. A biome is a particular part of the biosphere in which the climate, soils, and plant life are similar throughout.

6.3 Why Study Earth's Spheres Separately?

Sometimes it helps to understand how something works by taking it apart and studying each piece separately. If you want to know more about how your bicycle works, you could take off the wheels and the tires, take off the chain, and remove the sprockets to study each part by itself.

You might discover that your bicycle frame is built out of sturdy metal and that it is hollow inside to make it lighter. You might discover that your tire tubes are made out of soft rubber and the tires are thicker with small bumps or treads that help the tires grip the road. You might also discover that the chain is flexible and can bend and that a sprocket is hard and has teeth to support and carry the chain.

By studying each piece of your bike separately, you can better understand how your bike works when it's all put together.

The same is true about studying Earth. It's useful for geologists to look carefully at each sphere and learn everything they can about water or air or the rocks that make up Earth. Also, because there is so much to learn, no one person can study everything. This is one reason geologists specialize in different areas of geology. A geochemist may focus only on studying the water in the oceans, and a structural geologist may only study the mountains beneath the oceans. When they work together and swap information, they both understand the oceans better.

6.4 Putting Them All Together

Just like your whole bike functions as a combination of different parts working together, Earth operates as a combination of different parts that work together. The atmosphere, biosphere, geosphere, hydrosphere, and magnetosphere all work together to create the planet we call Earth.

For example, when the atmosphere creates a big storm over the ocean, the hydrosphere is affected, and the biosphere and geosphere may also be affected. When animals in the biosphere, like beavers and people, build dams, it can affect the geosphere, hydrosphere, and other parts of the biosphere. When a volcano erupts, it can affect the geosphere, atmosphere, and biosphere.

By studying the individual spheres separately and then pooling all that information to study Earth as a whole, geologists can gain a more accurate picture of this world we call Earth.

6.5 Summary

○ Earth can be studied as a combination of different spheres.

○ The five major spheres that make up Earth are the geosphere, atmosphere, biosphere, hydrosphere, and magnetosphere.

○ Studying each sphere separately helps scientists learn more about how they work.

○ Combining the information about each sphere into the study of Earth as a whole helps scientists gain a more accurate picture of Earth.

6.6 Some Things to Think About

○ What is your favorite sphere to study?

Geosphere (studying rocks and dirt)

Biosphere (studying plants and animals)

Hydrosphere (studying rivers and oceans)

Atmosphere (studying weather and clouds)

Magnetosphere (studying magnetic fields and solar storms)

○ Name some parts of Earth's spheres that are near where you live. (mountains, oceans, rivers, forests etc.)

○ Have you ever taken something apart to find out how it works? Describe what you found out.

○ Have you ever put something together and observed how it works as a whole? (For example, a bicycle, a Lego structure, or a robot) Describe what you found out.

Chapter 7 The Geosphere

7.1 Introduction

The term geosphere refers to the part of Earth that is made of rocks, minerals, and soils. The geosphere extends from the surface of Earth all the way to the very center. Geological activity occurs in the geosphere and includes earthquakes and volcanoes.

Scientists think the geosphere is made of several layers that are different from one another. One way to describe the geosphere is to divide it into three main layers: the crust, the mantle, and the core.

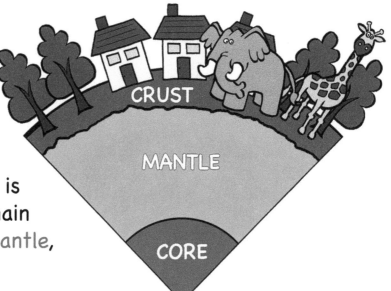

To create a more detailed picture of Earth's layers, geologists often subdivide the main layers of Earth into additional layers. This is helpful when more specific descriptions of the geosphere are needed. Scientists group and name the various layers in different ways according to what will be most helpful to them in studying the geosphere. There is no one right way to list Earth's layers. It just depends on what kinds of questions scientists want to answer.

7.2 More About Layers

Although scientists can use different names for the layers of the geosphere, in this book we will use the following names for the layers: the crust, the mantle (divided into the lithosphere, asthenosphere, and mesosphere), and the core (divided into the outer core and the inner core).

The crust is the outermost layer of Earth and is the part of the geosphere that we live on. The crust is hard and is made of rocks, soil, and minerals. The crust makes up mountains, the ocean floor, mesas, river beds, and other features.

Below the crust is the mantle, which is further subdivided into three layers called the lithosphere, asthenosphere, and mesosphere.

The lithosphere lies just below the crust and, like the crust, is a hard, rocky layer. Geologists believe the lithosphere is broken up into huge pieces called plates. It is thought that the lithosphere sits on top of a soft, putty-like layer called the asthenosphere which is made of molten (melted) rock called magma. Heat in the asthenosphere causes the magma in this layer to move. As the magma moves, it carries the plates of the lithosphere along with it, causing earthquakes and volcanoes as the plates shift and push against each other.

Below the asthenosphere is the mesosphere. The mesosphere makes up the largest part of the mantle. Scientists believe that the mesosphere is more solid than the asthenosphere.

Below the mesosphere and at the very center of Earth is the core. The core is divided into the outer core and the inner core. The outer core is thought to be made of liquid rock and metal, and the inner core is thought to be solid. Since it isn't possible to drill to the center of the Earth, geologists don't know exactly what the outer core and the inner core are like, but they can make educated guesses based on the data they collect from experiments.

It's good to keep in mind that scientists sometimes use different groupings and names for the layers of Earth. For example, sometimes the lithosphere and asthenosphere are grouped together and called the upper mantle with the mesosphere being called the lower mantle. And at other times, geologists may group the crust and lithosphere together into a layer they simply call the lithosphere.

7.3 Evidence and Guessing

There is much about the geosphere that geologists simply don't know. Because we have not been able to dig below the Earth's crust, we can't get samples of the Earth's interior. This means that some of the conclusions scientists make about how the

geosphere works are more like educated guesses.

An educated guess is a guess based on scientific information. When there is enough information to suggest that an educated guess is correct, the guess can become a scientific theory. Sometimes an educated guess is discarded when new evidence suggests that the idea is incorrect. Either way, we gain more understanding of how the geosphere works by looking at evidence, making educated guesses, developing theories, and then discarding theories and guesses when new information challenges old ideas.

For example, as we saw earlier, geologists have found evidence that supports the idea that the lithosphere is divided into plates and earthquakes are caused by the movement of these plates on the soft asthenosphere. Scientists also think that the magma in the asthenosphere can be forced through cracks or thin places in the lithosphere, causing volcanoes to erupt.

There is no way to actually sample the lithosphere or the asthenosphere, so geologists don't know for certain that the lithosphere is hard and the asthenosphere is soft and putty-like. However, they can use advanced tools to gather information, and based on that information they can make an educated guess about what the lithosphere and the asthenosphere are like.

7.4 The Geosphere and Other Spheres

The crust is one part of the geosphere that is affected directly by the other spheres, like the atmosphere, the biosphere, and the hydrosphere. The crust is shaped both by the lower layers of Earth where earthquakes and volcanoes begin and by wind, rain, storms, and animals.

For example, a volcano might erupt and create a tall mountain. Over time the mountain may erode and become smaller and smaller because of wind and rain. An earthquake may occur, creating a new passageway for water, and animals might build their homes in the new waterway, creating small ponds or lakes.

The magnetic field that surrounds Earth is believed to be created by the motion of liquid metals in the outer core. If Earth didn't have a core made mostly of metals, we would not have a magnetic field to form the magnetosphere.

The lower layers of the geosphere are not directly affected by the other spheres of the Earth. It doesn't rain on the asthenosphere, and animals can't dig homes in the mesosphere.

7.5 Summary

○ The geosphere includes all the rock parts of Earth and extends from the surface of Earth all the way to the very center.

○ The geosphere can be divided into three main layers: crust, mantle, and core. These main layers can be further subdivided into more layers.

○ Geologists can only take samples of the outermost layer of the geosphere (the crust) and have to make educated guesses about the inner layers.

○ The crust is the layer of the geosphere most affected by other spheres.

7.6 Some Things to Think About

○ Have you ever created a layered cake or dessert? Describe what you did and what it looked like.

○ Do you think we'll ever be able to drill to the Earth's core? Why or why not?

○ How would you explain in your own words how scientists use evidence to make educated guesses

○ How do you think animals change Earth's crust?

Chapter 8 The Air We Breathe

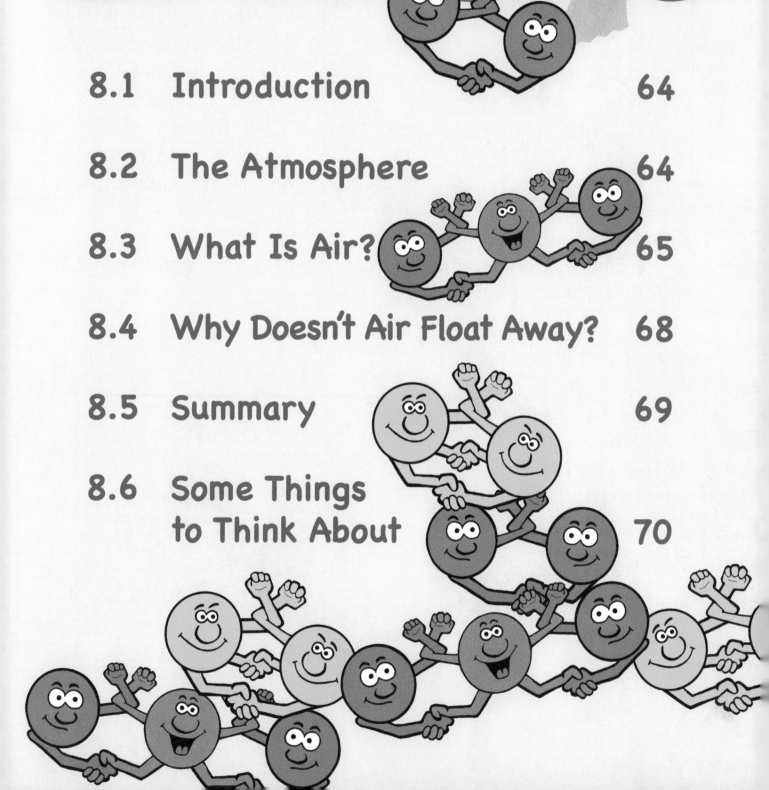

8.1 Introduction

Notice what happens when you breathe. Take a deep breath in. What is going into your lungs? Exhale. What comes out?

Air is the name for what we breathe in and what we breathe out. We live on a planet that has the kind of air needed for life. Without the air on Earth, there wouldn't be animals on farms, ponds full of fish, or forests full of trees.

8.2 The Atmosphere

The air we breathe exists in the part of the Earth that scientists call the atmosphere. The atmosphere sits just above the Earth's crust and extends for several miles above the surface.

Earth is the only planet in our solar system that has an atmosphere suitable for life as we know it.

Most of the time we don't think too much about the air that surrounds us. We breathe it in and we exhale it out as we go about our day. Some people, though, live in areas where the air is not clean. In some areas of the world, the air contains so much pollution, or small particles, that it is difficult to breathe. Knowing about the air, what it is, and how to keep it clean is important to all living things on Earth.

8.3 What Is Air?

You might think most of the air we breathe is oxygen. But it isn't. The air we breathe is a mixture of different gas molecules and water vapor. Air has nitrogen gas, oxygen gas, carbon dioxide gas, a little bit of argon gas, and some water vapor.

Nitrogen gas in the air exists as a molecule with two nitrogen atoms hooked together. When you breathe, nitrogen gas goes inside your lungs and comes out again when you exhale. Your body doesn't use nitrogen gas. It only uses oxygen gas.

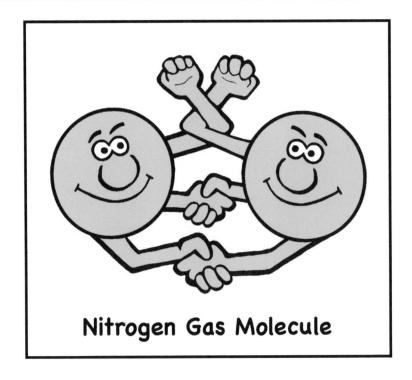

Nitrogen Gas Molecule

You have probably heard that you need oxygen to stay alive. In fact, if you hold your breath too long, you will pass out and your body will automatically start breathing again to keep you alive. Oxygen is more important than food or water, and you can't stay alive very long without it.

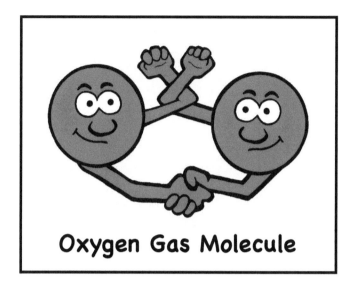

Oxygen Gas Molecule

Oxygen gas is made of two oxygen atoms hooked together. When you breathe in, your lungs expand and oxygen gas goes inside.

Lungs have special cells that absorb oxygen from the air and deliver it to your blood. Your blood has special molecules that then carry the oxygen to the rest of your body. Your body uses the oxygen to process food and give you energy.

After our bodies use the oxygen we have inhaled, they make carbon dioxide gas. Carbon dioxide gas is made of one carbon atom and two oxygen atoms hooked together. When you exhale, you breathe out the carbon dioxide gas.

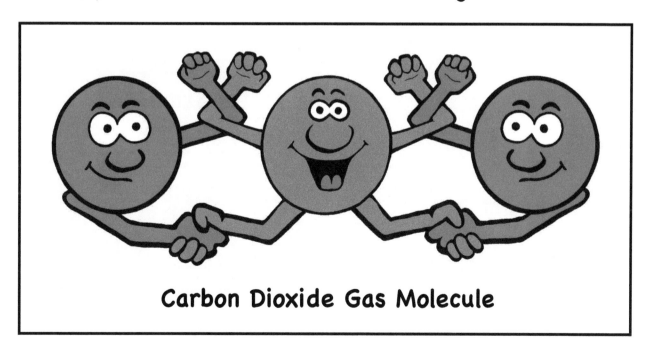

Carbon Dioxide Gas Molecule

This works out great because plants use carbon dioxide to make the food that allows them to stay alive and grow. Plants take in carbon dioxide and then put oxygen back into the air. We help plants and plants help us!

8.4 Why Doesn't Air Float Away?

You might have wondered if there is oxygen, nitrogen, or carbon dioxide in space. In fact, when astronauts travel outside our atmosphere and into space, they have to wear a special suit so they can have oxygen to breathe.

But what keeps the air we breathe close to the Earth, and why doesn't it just all float away into space? In fact, what keeps you on the Earth, and why don't you float away?

You don't float away for the same reason the air in our atmosphere doesn't float away. Gravity keeps you on the ground and keeps the air we breathe close to the Earth's surface. Gravity is a force that pulls everything near the Earth toward its center. Go ahead and try to jump off the Earth. As soon as you jump up, you will feel Earth's gravity pulling you back down again.

8.5 Summary

○ The air we breathe is in the Earth's atmosphere.

○ The air we breathe is made up of nitrogen gas, oxygen gas, carbon dioxide gas, argon gas, and water vapor.

○ Our bodies inhale air, use the oxygen, and then exhale carbon dioxide gas.

○ Gravity keeps the air from floating away into space.

8.5 Some Things to Think About

○ What does your breath look like on a cold winter day? Why do you think you can see your breath?

○ What do you think would happen to all the plants and animals if our atmosphere disappeared?

○ What do you think would happen if all the plants disappeared?

○ If you jumped hard enough, do you think you could jump off the Earth? Why or why not?

Chapter 9 Our Water

9.1 Introduction

Do you ever play in the rain and wonder how the water got into the clouds? Have you watched water flowing in a river and wondered where it comes from and where it goes? Have you ever noticed that ocean water is salty and lake water is not and then wondered why this is so?

Water is very important for life on Earth. Without water, life could not exist. Geologists study water and how it travels around the Earth.

9.2 Hydrosphere

The hydrosphere is the name for the water part of Earth. All the water on Earth makes up the hydrosphere. The hydrosphere includes all the water in lakes, rivers, and the oceans. It also includes rain, ice, snow, and the water in clouds and in the ground.

Water exists in three forms—as a liquid (flowing water), as a solid (ice and snow), and as water vapor (in the clouds). Part of the way water moves around the Earth is by changing from one form to another. Liquid water in oceans, lakes, and rivers evaporates, or changes from its liquid form to water vapor, which is water's gaseous form.

When liquid water freezes to become ice and snow, the water changes to its solid form. When ice and snow melt, water returns to its liquid form.

9.3 The Water Cycle

The way water moves around Earth is called a cycle. Recall that a cycle is a series of events that repeat. We can think of the water cycle as beginning when liquid water flows from rivers into the oceans and then evaporates. Evaporation puts water into the atmosphere where it forms clouds. Then rain on the land puts the water back into the rivers. The cycle begins over again when this river water flows into the oceans.

9.4 Earth Is a Water Planet

How much water is on the Earth? If you look at a globe or a map of the Earth, you will see that oceans cover most of the planet. In fact, oceans cover almost 3/4 of Earth's surface!

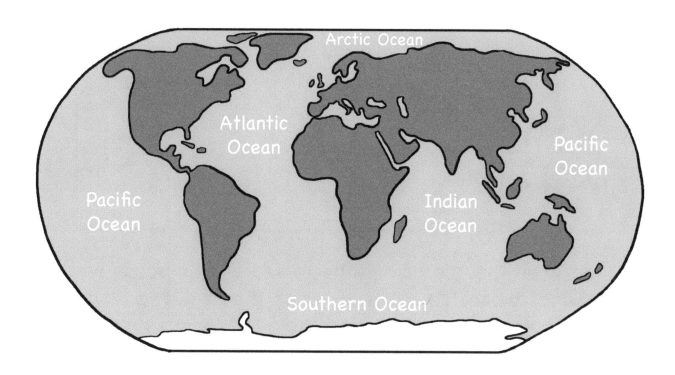

Oceans are very important for life on Earth. In addition to providing evaporated water that can fall as rain or snow, oceans absorb heat from the Sun. Ocean water is constantly moving around the Earth and carries this heat around the globe, keeping Earth from getting too cold.

The oceans gradually release into the atmosphere the heat they got from the Sun. This warms the air above the oceans. Winds blow the warmed air over the land, which warms the land.

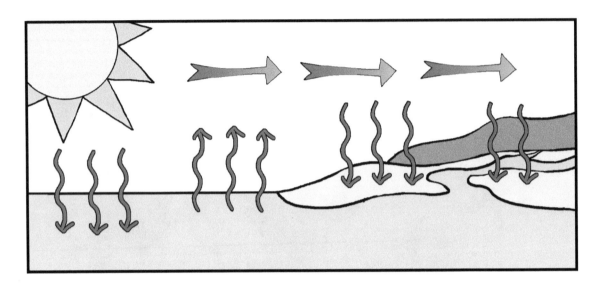

Also, air over the oceans may be cooled by the ocean water. When winds blow this cooler air over the land, the land is cooled and kept from getting too hot. The oceans have a big effect on temperature and weather on the Earth.

Even though the oceans contain so much water, the water is not good for drinking—it is much too salty to drink. The salts in the oceans come from rocks. Tiny bits of rocks are worn away from big rocks by rain, wind, and moving water. These very tiny rock bits are carried by rivers to the oceans and make the ocean water salty.

9.5 Water on the Land

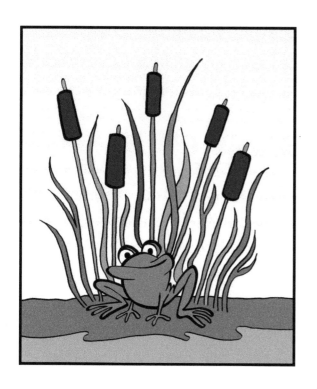

Surface water is the name for the water that is on top of the land. Surface water is found in lakes, rivers, streams, swamps, and marshes. Surface water is very important for life. Animals and plants would not be able to live without water.

9.6 Water in the Ground

Water that is under the Earth's surface is called groundwater. When it rains or snows, some of the rain or snow seeps down into the ground. Plants can take up this water through their roots and use it to stay alive and grow.

There are some places in the ground that hold lots of water. Wells pump this water to the surface where it can be used for drinking and other purposes, such as farming.

9.7 Keeping Our Water Clean

The same water is used over and over on Earth. The same water will sometimes be in the oceans, sometimes on the land or in the ground, and sometimes in the atmosphere. The same water keeps changing between its liquid, solid, and gaseous forms and keeps moving around the Earth.

Without clean water, life could not exist on Earth. Since we use the same water over and over, it's important to keep it clean. But people are not always careful to keep our water clean. They throw trash and chemicals into rivers and the oceans.

Also, smoke from factory smokestacks and exhaust from cars can dirty, or pollute, the air in the atmosphere. This pollution mixes with water vapor in the clouds and falls to Earth as rain or snow. If there is enough pollution, it can make plants and animals sick.

Geologists and other scientists are studying pollution to find out how we can change the way we do things so that we can keep our water and air clean.

9.8 Summary

○ The water part of Earth is called the hydrosphere.

○ Water exists in three forms: liquid, solid (ice and snow), and gas (water vapor).

○ Water moves around the Earth in a cycle, or series of events that repeat.

○ Oceans hold most of the Earth's water.

○ **Surface water** is water that is on top of the land, and **groundwater** is water that is under Earth's surface.

○ Clean water is important for life to exist.

9.9 Some Things to Think About

○ What are some ways you have observed that water moves from one place to another?

○ What do you think are some ways that you can get water to change from one form to another?

○ How do you think snow that falls in the winter fits into the water cycle?

○ How do you think the oceans are helpful to life on Earth?

○ Where would you find surface water near your house?

○ Where do you think you would find groundwater near your house?

○ What are some things you think you could do to help keep water clean?

Chapter 10 Plants and Animals

10.1 Introduction

Earth is not made of just rocks, water, and air. Earth has trees, frogs, butterflies, rabbits, deer, and worms. Earth is the only place we know of that has living things. The living things on Earth make up what is known as the biosphere.

The biosphere contains all living things and every place where life can exist on Earth. The biosphere includes plants, animals, and bugs, and also the land, the water on the land, the oceans, the part of the atmosphere near Earth, and even some underground places.

Different parts of the biosphere work together to help support life. For example, the soil provides the water and nutrients plants need to live. Animals use plants for food and they drink water. Birds fly in the atmosphere to catch bugs for food. Plants and animals get the carbon dioxide and oxygen they need from the atmosphere.

10.2 Cycles

Water is not the only resource on Earth that is used over and over again. There are also different elements (atoms) that are used repeatedly by living things in the biosphere.

The elements carbon and oxygen are used over and over again in a carbon-oxygen cycle. Think about the oxygen we and other animals breathe in from the atmosphere. We inhale oxygen atoms that we use to power our bodies. We breathe out carbon dioxide.

Plants use carbon atoms from carbon dioxide to make food and then release oxygen atoms back into the air where animals breathe them in again. In the carbon-oxygen cycle, both oxygen atoms and carbon atoms are used over and over.

Nitrogen also has a cycle. In the nitrogen cycle, nitrogen from the atmosphere goes into the soil where bacteria change the nitrogen into a form that plants can use. This process is called "fixing" the nitrogen. Plants absorb the "fixed" nitrogen with their roots and use it to grow. Animals eat the plants and use the nitrogen from the plants to make proteins and run the machinery inside their cells.

Without the carbon-oxygen cycle and the nitrogen cycle plants and animals would not be able to live.

10.3 The Sun

Do you know how animals get energy from the Sun? By eating plants! When sunlight shines on plants, the plants use the sunlight to make the sugars they use for their own food. When animals eat the plants, they get energy from the Sun by using the sugars that the plants made from sunlight.

10.4 Environment

An environment is everything that surrounds a living thing in the area where it lives. Water, weather, soils, plants, and animals are all part of an environment.

Scientists study how all the different parts of an environment affect each other. How much water do the plants in a particular area need to have in order to grow? Which plants will certain animals eat? Which living things exist in environments that are hot and dry? Which ones live where it is cold or wet?

Learning about different environments helps scientists understand what resources are needed for plants and animals in a specific area to grow and be healthy.

10.5 Summary

○ The biosphere is the living part of Earth and contains all the living things on Earth.

○ Different parts of the biosphere work together to help support life.

○ Living things in the biosphere use oxygen, carbon, and nitrogen atoms in cycles that repeat over and over.

○ Animals get energy from the Sun by eating plants.

○ An environment includes everything that surrounds a living thing in the area where it lives.

10.6 Some Things to Think About

○ What is your favorite part of the biosphere?

Fish in the ocean

Birds in the air

Plants in the garden

Wild animals in the forest

Lizards in the desert

Worms in the soil

Bats in a cave

Lily pads in a pond

Some other part

○ What do you think would happen to animals if there were no bacteria in the soil to "fix" nitrogen? Why?

○ What do you think would happen if we could not eat plants?

○ Do you think changes in the hydrosphere can affect environments in the biosphere?

Chapter 11 Magnetic Earth

11.1 Introduction

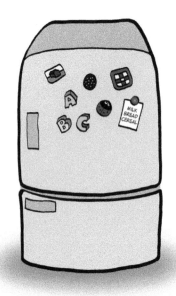

Have you ever noticed how a refrigerator magnet sticks to metal things? Have you played with a compass and observed how the needle always points in the same direction? Have you played with two bar magnets and observed how the opposite poles of the magnets will stick together and the same poles will not? All of these events occur because of magnetic forces.

11.2 Magnets Have Fields

A magnet is a particular kind of metal that can create magnetic forces. Magnetic forces allow a magnet to attract certain types of metals to it. Magnetic forces surround a magnet in what is called a magnetic field.

Magnets have poles, or opposite ends. The poles in a magnet occur because the magnetic forces are going in opposite directions. The north pole of a magnet is where the magnetic field points outward, and the south pole is where the magnetic field points inward.

If you have two magnets, you can find out which of their two poles are the same and which are different. The poles that are the same will repel each other (push each other apart). The poles that are different will attract each other and stick together.

11.3 Earth Is a Magnet!

North Pole

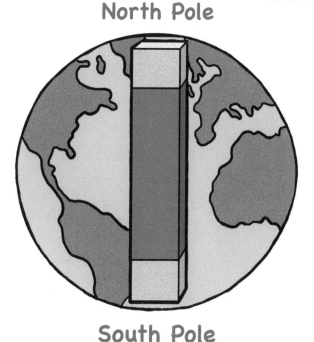

South Pole

It's hard to believe, but Earth is a gigantic magnet with a north pole and a south pole! You might think about Earth being a magnet by imagining a huge bar magnet going through the center of Earth from the top to the bottom. The top end of Earth's magnet is at the North Pole and the bottom end is at the South Pole.

The outer part of Earth's core is made of molten iron and nickel. Scientists think this molten part of Earth's core swirls around, creating a magnetic force. This magnetic force surrounds the Earth in a magnetic field.

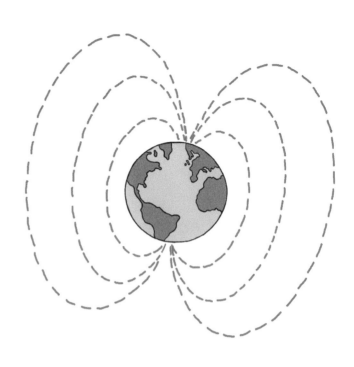

Did you know that you can use Earth's magnetic field to find your way out of the woods? When you use a compass, the magnetic needle in the compass is attracted to the Earth's North Pole, so the needle always points to the north.

11.4 Earth's Magnetic Field in Space

Earth's magnetic field extends into space and is affected by heat and light energy sent out by the Sun. This energy is called solar wind. Earth's magnetosphere is formed when the solar wind hits the magnetic field.

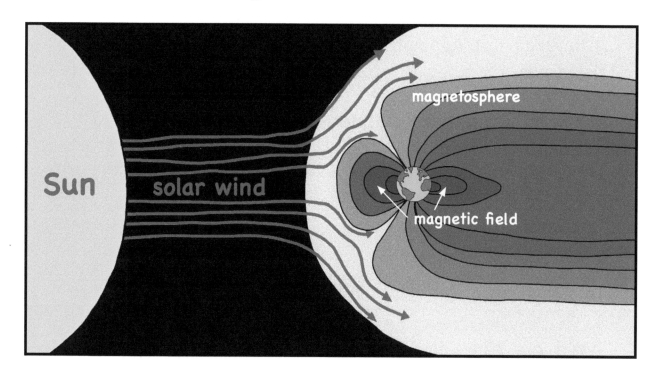

Plants and animals need heat and light energy from the Sun in order to live and grow. But too much of this energy would be harmful to life. The magnetosphere protects life on Earth by letting just enough energy get through. The excess energy is stopped by the magnetosphere. This extra energy then slides around the magnetosphere and continues on into space.

11.5 Summary

○ A magnet is a certain type of metal that can attract certain other metals.

○ Magnetic force allows a magnet to attract other metals.

○ A magnet has opposite poles called the north pole and the south pole.

○ Earth is like a giant magnet.

○ The magnetosphere contains Earth's magnetic field and protects Earth from getting too much energy from the Sun.

11.6 Some Things to Think About

○ What are some things that you think magnets can be used for?

○ What do you think would happen if all metals had magnetic fields?

○ How do you think discovery of Earth's magnetic field changed the way people could travel?

○ Look at the illustration of the magnetosphere. Why do you think the magnetosphere is short on the side facing the Sun and long on the side away from the Sun?

Chapter 12 Working Together

12.1 Introduction

Did you know that all the parts of Earth depend on each other? Without the atmosphere, plants and animals in the biosphere could not get the oxygen and carbon dioxide they need to live, and there would be no rain to bring them water. Without water from the hydrosphere, the cells that make up plants and animals could not produce oxygen

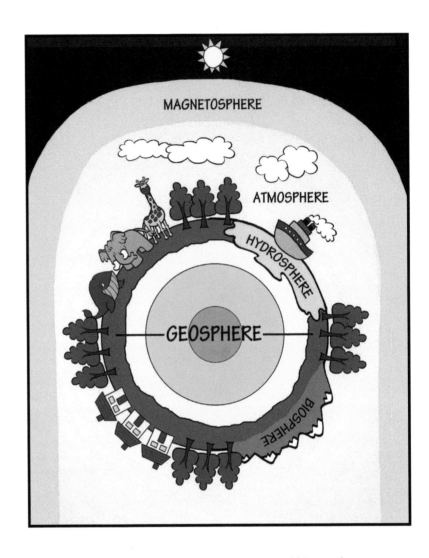

and carbon dioxide to go into the atmosphere. Without the swirling of iron and nickel in Earth's geosphere, there would be no magnetosphere. Without the magnetosphere, plants and animals would get too much energy from the Sun and would die.

12.2 Earth as a Whole

All of the parts of Earth fit together in just the right way, like a big puzzle. In order for Earth to function as a whole, it needs all of the pieces to be in place.

The geosphere, biosphere, hydrosphere, atmosphere, and magnetosphere all work together to make up what we know as Earth. All of the parts of Earth depend on each other. In order to grow and live, you depend on members of your family and members of your community. In a similar way, all the parts of Earth depend on each other to keep Earth working. If you were to take away any one part, Earth as we know it wouldn't exist.

12.3 Earth in Balance

Earth's parts are in balance with each other. There is enough liquid water and water vapor for rivers, oceans, clouds, and rain. There are enough plants to produce oxygen for animals and enough animals to make carbon dioxide for plants. There is enough of the Sun's energy for plants to grow and a strong enough magnetosphere to block excess energy from the Sun.

However, it is possible to throw Earth off balance. If too much carbon dioxide were in the atmosphere and there weren't enough plants to change it to oxygen, the Earth's climate would change. As a result, the Earth would become too warm or too cold. If too much liquid water were stored as ice, there would be less water in the oceans and they might not be able to support life. If too much ice melted, weather patterns could change, making some parts of Earth too wet and some parts too dry, some parts too hot and some parts too cold.

12.4 How Can We Help?

Keeping Earth in balance is important for life. Many of Earth's cycles can adjust to small changes, but if the changes were to get too big, Earth's cycles could begin to work differently from the way they do now. Scientists don't understand everything about how Earth's cycles work, and they don't know everything about how to keep Earth in balance.

Humans can both help and hurt Earth's balance. For example, humans make some chemicals that can create problems for plants and animals. If too many chemicals are in the environment, plants and animals can die. But if humans clean up the harmful chemicals and replace them with ones that are not harmful to living things, the plants and animals will have a better chance of staying healthy.

Humans also use products, such as plastics, that can create problems when a lot of them get into the oceans. Scientists are trying to discover how to make materials that could be used like plastics but would be changed into harmless substances after being used. This would be a great step toward keeping the oceans clean.

Scientists are working on many new ideas that could help keep our planet healthy and in balance. Maybe you will come up with the next great idea!

12.5 Summary

○ All of Earth's parts work together.

○ The atmosphere, biosphere, hydrosphere, geosphere, and magnetosphere all depend on each other.

○ Earth stays in balance naturally.

○ Human activity can change Earth's balance.

12.6 Some Things to Think About

○ Think of one of Earth's parts. If it stopped working, how would the other parts be affected?

○ Why do you think it can be difficult for scientists to predict exactly how a change in one part of Earth will affect other parts of Earth?

○ How do you think the different parts of Earth stay in balance? How might they get out of balance?

○ What are some things you can do to keep Earth healthy?

○ What new idea do you have that could be used to keep Earth healthy?

Glossary-Index

dirt • see soil

earthquake • a shaking of Earth that happens when sections of the crust move suddenly, 7, 15, 33, 38, 39, 43-44, 55, 57, 59, 60

educated guess • a guess or idea based on scientific data, 57-60

element (E-luh-ment) • an atom, 21, 84

environment (in-VYE-run-ment) • everything that surrounds a living thing in the area where it lives, 6, 86-87, 99

environmental geologist • see geologist, environmental

equator (i-KWAY-ter) • the part of Earth halfway between the North Pole and the South Pole, 30, 31

evaporate (i-VAP-uh-rate) • to change from a liquid to a gas, 73, 74, 75

fixing • in geology, the process by which bacteria change nitrogen in the soil into a form that can be used by plants, 85

geochemist (jee-oh-KE-mist) • a geologist who studies the chemistry of Earth, 5, 51

geographic information system (jee-uh-GRA-fik in-for-MAY-shun SIS-tum) (GIS) • a computer system that is used to gather and analyze geographical data, 15

geologist (jee-AH-luh-jist) • a scientist who studies the Earth, 5

geologist, environmental (jee-AH-luh-jist, in-vie-run-MEN-tul) • a geologist who studies Earth's environment, 6

geologist, structural (jee-AH-luh-jist, STRUK-chuh-rul) • a geologist who studies how Earth is put together and how it changes, 6, 51

geology (jee-AH-luh-jee) • the study of Earth, 2

geosphere (JEE-oh-sfir) • Earth's crust, mantle, and core together; made of rock, minerals, and soils, 35, 47, 48, 49, 51-52, 55-61, 96-100

GIS • geographic information system, 15

global positioning system (GPS) (GLOE-bul puh-ZI-shuh-ning SIS-tum) • an electronic device that uses signals from satellites to determine position on Earth, 14

GPS • global positioning system, 14

gravity (GRA-vuh-tee) • the force that pulls everything on or near Earth toward the center of Earth, 69

groundwater • water that is below the surface of Earth, 77

guess, educated • see educated guess

hammer, chisel edge rock • a hammer that has a head with one flat, square end and one broad, chisel-like end; used to break rocks, 11, 12, 13

south pole • the end of a magnet where the magnetic field points inward, 91

South Pole • the very bottom point on Earth, 30, 31, 91-92

sphere (sfir) • a ball-shaped object; in geology, one of several parts of the Earth that work together, 47-52

structural geologist • see geologist, structural

surface water • water that is on top of land, 77

technology (tek-NAH-luh-jee) • a machine or piece of equipment developed by using scientific knowledge to solve a problem, 14

Theophrastus (thee-uh-FRA-stus) • [371-287 BCE] Greek philosopher; one of the first people to study Earth's features and rocks, 4, 11

upper mantle • see mantle, upper

volcano (vol-KAY-noe) • an eruption of molten rock caused by pressure forcing magma through a weak spot in the crust, 15, 33, 38-42, 52, 55, 57, 59, 60

volcano (vol-KAY-noe), **cone** • a steep-sided, cone-shaped volcano that forms quickly, 41-42

volcano, shield (vol-KAY-noe, SHEELD) • a volcano with long, sloping sides formed over a long period of time, 41, 42

water cycle (SYE-kul) • the way water moves around Earth, 74-76

water vapor (VAY-pur) • the gaseous state of water, 65, 73, 78, 98

More REAL SCIENCE-4-KIDS Books
by Rebecca W. Keller, PhD

Building Blocks Series
yearlong study program — each Student Textbook has accompanying Laboratory Notebook, Teacher's Manual, Lesson Plan, Study Notebook, Quizzes, and Graphics Package

Exploring the Building Blocks of Science Book K (Activity Book)
Exploring the Building Blocks of Science Book 1
Exploring the Building Blocks of Science Book 2
Exploring the Building Blocks of Science Book 3
Exploring the Building Blocks of Science Book 4
Exploring the Building Blocks of Science Book 5
Exploring the Building Blocks of Science Book 6
Exploring the Building Blocks of Science Book 7
Exploring the Building Blocks of Science Book 8

Focus Series
unit study program — each title has a Student Textbook with accompanying Laboratory Notebook, Teacher's Manual, Lesson Plan, Study Notebook, Quizzes, and Graphics Package

Focus On Elementary Chemistry
Focus On Elementary Biology
Focus On Elementary Physics
Focus On Elementary Geology
Focus On Elementary Astronomy

Focus On Middle School Chemistry
Focus On Middle School Biology
Focus On Middle School Physics
Focus On Middle School Geology
Focus On Middle School Astronomy

Focus On High School Chemistry

Super Simple Science Experiments

21 Super Simple Chemistry Experiments
21 Super Simple Biology Experiments
21 Super Simple Physics Experiments
21 Super Simple Geology Experiments
21 Super Simple Astronomy Experiments
101 Super Simple Science Experiments

Note: A few titles may still be in production.

Gravitas Publications Inc.
www.gravitaspublications.com
www.realscience4kids.com

GRAVITAS
PUBLICATIONS

CPSIA information can be obtained
at www.ICGtesting.com
Printed in the USA
BVHW022004220819
556561BV00027BA/6620/P